To contact the author, send an email to
matfigueroa12@gmail.com

To my parents, for giving me life (and free food on the weekends)

To Laurie Cahill, for giving me hope

To my friends, for giving me a home in their hearts

To my brother, Tom, for always pushing me to be more than what I am

To my cousin, Jon, for always believing in me even when I can't find reasons to

To God, for keeping me alive long enough to understand that there is more to this journey than pain. For blessing me with the ability to shape my demons into a means of connecting with others through words. And, for bathing me in light no matter how much I once hated or shunned You for the dark.

High School Mat

Could always relate to words better than people. It's amazing how they unite to birth stories that, simply put, make you feel sh!t.

For a long time, I was uncomfortable in my own skin, slave to panic attacks and depression. I bottled everything up, believing something was wrong with me; that it was MY fault. Trying to talk about it made matters worse, as no one believed the existence or the extent of my issues.

Writing helped me navigate my emotions when I was drowning in them, and speaking those words brought a unique joy. Few things are more exhilarating than telling a story—the act of opening your heart to your community.

I use my words to share my pain, and let others know that they aren't alone.

P.S.—"Pizzeria Uno is for Winners, and Ham Sandwiches are for Losers"

Contents

Let's go back in time...

Don't worry

We won't stay there long

MY ANXIETY...

Is the iceberg that sank the Titanic

Puts the hopeless
In Instagram scrolling romantics

Increases the power dynamic of panic
To attack! Whenever I see people

Dammit

You are the boulder Sisyphus was handed
No matter how far he pushed
You rolled back to where you started

You're not immovable
You just make progress impossible

11

LIKE LIGHT

She bends

In different directions

Depending on who's looking

From which angle

Straining to sustain

The different perceptions

Of friends and family

Ignoring her inner perspective

And any sense of

"Me"

REASONS I SHOULD HANG ON

Maybe

This mood will change

Like the seasons

Fade like fall leaves

Be rejected like spring sneezes

Jesus

How did you hang on?

Suspended there Your back against

The cross. Blood loss from the thorns

Piercing your skull you loved people

Who hated you who cheered as your

Skin turned pale and blue. I wanna say,

"If you held on then I can, too"

But I promised to never lie to You

I'm on the edge, fingers slipping

Cus deep down I want them to

Reasons I should hang on?

Because falling would make me happy

And I *always* sabotage my happiness

I was trapped in limbo; contemplating suicide because it was too much being alive, yet knowing I would never take that step, or slit, because of my Catholic school years. I wasn't saved through faith (not yet). Teachers drilled into our heads that suicide = eternal damnation, a fate further reinforced by the movie "Constantine". As much as I wanted to leave, I didn't see the point of suffering in worse ways for eternity. I hung on, no matter how much I wanted to fall. Looking back, perhaps the greater purpose behind being raised in a Catholic belief system was to keep me from taking that step?

God's Plan, huh?

"TRUTH"

You reject Love

And accept Hate

For surely,

Everyone

Must be as

Disgusted

With yourself

As you are

---

*I think a big component of depression is obsession
with the belief that you don't deserve peace or
happiness. I pushed away those who saw good in
my spirit, believing they were telling lies; yet
accepted those who reinforced my skewed self-
worth, treasuring their abuse as honesty.*

DEPENDENCE

You gave the dead parts of me life

And I mistook that for love it

Was all about what you

Could do for me and

Never what I

Could do

For you

---

*In relationships, I dumped all my woes onto my
significant other, finding peace in her embrace as it
gave me someplace to be other than home.
However, many of these women were suffering, too.
I belittled their struggles, putting mine on a grand
pedestal. This is far too late, but…I'm sorry.*

You all deserved better

Status Quo

Part 1

It dances on our tongues

[L O V E]

Wishing to be released

But we're afraid to change

The Status Quo

Part 2

We dance around the topic

Like crackling embers in the fireplace

Water long since poured

On our flame

Shame

How best friends

Can become lovers, then

Strangers

A moment of silence to the friends turned exes, lost in the sea of awkwardness post break-up. Was it worth it?

SENIOR YEAR

I'm sorry

To the women

Who felt played

After we shared a bed

And the weeks that followed

Without so much as a single text

I didn't want to be with you

I just didn't want to be alone

I thought catching bodies made me the man. However, it made me everything but a man. I was a boy, terrified of the desolation that accompanied an empty bed, with nothing to wrap my arms around but a pillow and my demons.

THE PARENT TRAP

The real parent trap is living

Your life according to

Their expectations

Parents are tasked with guiding us. For the most part (not always), they only want what's best for us. The disconnect is in the difference between our values, creating two contrasting definitions of "what's best". Don't be arrogant—heed the advice of your elders. However, only YOU know what's truly right for YOU. I'd much rather have someone disappointed in the choices I made, than live with regret for the ones I didn't.

HELP

A lot of shit went down growing up

Whenever I try to talk about it

Your pupils dilate

lips tremble

You fire back:

*"That was your father! I didn't do
anything."*

Mom...

That was the problem

SILENCE

Momma

A part of me wishes

We could turn back time

To when we'd talk for hours

About blissful nothings

Watching melanin soaked sitcoms

On UPN 9

Letting the television

Drown out our empty

Or maybe fill it up

While we commented on lives

That weren't real

And offered them advice

We ourselves would never follow

I guess,

The writing was always

On the wall

Momma

Some days I get so distraught

Cus you never wanna speak

About the past

So, many days I'd rather

Not speak to you at all

I don't think it's wrong

But I know it isn't right, either

It's just that I'm carrying

So much on my back I need you

To help me unpack & understand

If I am to be a better man than my father

And not be swallowed by

All this pain that isn't mine

Yet still hurts me, nonetheless

I'm talkin' bout these cycles

That have us vexed

Cus no one wants to check them

With words

People fear accountability

So they ignore the responsibility

They have to their own stories

Letting them become grim tales

That leach off their legacy

The next generation

Momma

It feels like this poetry is all I have

You're content burying the past

Pretending it never happened

Or misremembering the plot twist

Calling that last day of vacation in '96

A sunset happy ending

When in fact the genre shifted

From feel good family hit

To twisted psychological thriller

I'm not sure,

If the kids ever made it out

Momma

It feels like this poetry is my only chance

Of getting someone to sit and listen

To my grief

You have always worried

About my voice

And the "secrets" (aka truth)

It spills to strangers

About family business

Claiming it isn't my place

That I'm acting out and

Need to grow the fuck up

My word choice isn't about hate

I need to talk to someone about these things

Or they'll drive me insane

The fam is too tight lipped

And therapy isn't a fee

I care to pay

So the pen

Is all I have

The only thing between

Me and the cliff

That being said

I miss our friendship

If we could just talk

About these things

Candidly, at length

Wrap it up with a

Lil' Q & A

I'd relinquish the pen

And never pick it up again

I'd keep every secret between us

I just

Want to know

How things

Got so bad

Momma

Your silence

Doesn't make you a hero

Your silence

Doesn't make you a good wife

Biting your tongue until it bleeds

Your silence

Is a disease

That has brother so angry

He doesn't even see

The wrath shaping his path

As my sadness

Continues to surpass infinity

Momma

We're not asking for a solution

We just want you to

Acknowledge the burden

Your silence

And your husband's actions

Placed on your children

Instead

Of pretending

Everything

Is picture perfect

And our problems

Don't exist

I resented my mom for a long time. As I got older and learned about her lack of a father figure, I understood her emphasis on having a man in the home.

No matter what happened, she'd say things like "at least you know your father" or "at least he comes home to you every night".

She's a victim of her past, pulling from the present to fill a hole. Mother can't acknowledge the truth because she'd have to acknowledge her role in the abuse, and the weight of that guilt would destroy her. So, she pushes all that shit down.

She doesn't get a free pass, but...I get it. I was able to release much of my anger. At her, and at myself for not being able to save her.

WEEKENDS

My Depression

Is a blanket

In winter

Too thin

To keep me warm

But too heavy to move

I lay there

Silently accepting

That warmth is impossible

When you've been suffering for a long period, your problems become a core part of your identity. Depression was/is/was/is/was/is addictive, and I couldn't imagine myself without it. I NEEDED it. Change = scary unknowns, and humans are always more comfortable with "the devil they know".

HAM SANDWICHES

Back in the day
Before I was born when
The fam held hands with poverty
Friday nights were special
The one day they'd eat a
Delicacy—cold cuts from the deli
Ham sandwiches were fancy
And my father, the boyfriend, laughed

Fast forward to the first high school
Basketball game my girlfriend
Came to see me play
In the car pre-game we
Discussed dinner plans for after
Dad politely explained,
"Pizzeria Uno is for Winners, and
Ham Sandwiches are for Losers"

We lost the game
…know what happened next?

We drove past the restaurant and
Ate ham sandwiches at home
In silence
As usual, I blamed
Myself for being
Such a fuckin'
Loser

"DON'T TOUCH"

I'm Claustrophobic
Shuddering
At your tight embrace
I want you close, but
I'm screaming for space
It's how I was raised

Distance = Safe
   Close = Pain

Cus love only led
To daily disappointment
And hugs were for whispering
Lies onto my shoulder

It was the people I loved who hurt me the most. My anxiety eventually spiraled out of control, fueling the paranoia that ALL whom I love will hurt me. Thus, I was always "ready" for betrayal, accepting it as basic human nature. Even from friends. I guess, I didn't really trust them. Never gave 'em a fair chance.

    "Congratulations. You played yourself"

PERFECTIONISTS

I scored 20 points

"But you missed 2 free throws"

I got an A

"What about the plus?"

I have a girlfriend

"But she lives in the projects"

I'm giving a speech in assembly

"Don't fuck it up with your mumbling"

I made honors

"That's an <u>expectation</u>, not an achievement"

Even now, my victories don't always feel like accomplishments. I feel like I'm not doing enough; that I should be doing much more. To the parents, THIS is not encouragement. This sends the message that our successes will always be inadequate, so we try out failure. We fall in love with life without expectations; with life without goals we will always fall short of. Failure doesn't judge. It accepts us as we are

LEGACY

I learned about a bird

That scientists are

Raising then releasing

To help them repopulate

They only need to be taught their

Migratory flight pattern once

Then this habit is ingrained

In future generations

As instinct

The children become defined

By behaviors their parents

Couldn't help but follow

Trapped in cycles they didn't

Choose or understand

I wonder if

These demons are

Really mine or just

Another thing you gave me ?

Pain breeds cycles in our communities. A chunk of it revolves around <u>Love</u>*. Because they didn't get the proper nurturing from their family, men/women/boys/girls quest after a "perfect image" of companionship & affection vs seeking the right person, often ending up with an incompatible partner. Then, if shit gets wild between yall and the family structure deteriorates, the child misses out on the same things the parents did, spurring his/her odyssey for love & affection in all the wrong places, and so on...*

MR. GLASS

When you've shattered to pieces

More times than numbers go

You learn that it's useless putting yourself

Back together the same way

Cus it's only a matter of

Weeks   Days   Minutes

Until you break again

You learn how to

Spread out the different pieces

So that when one falls

There won't be a domino effect

So that when one part of you dies

The decay won't spread

There's a word for that

It's called, Resilience

And I took pride in my strength

I took pride in being

Resilient

The morning Grandma died

The hospital called and you'd think they sent

Shards of glass through the receiver the way

Mother clutched her head and howled

Howled the way Simba did

When his pops got stomped

Howled the way Eric did

When he couldn't draw breath

I don't mean it was loud

I mean it sounded like death

They both knew they were losing something

For good and no matter how much they struggled

It was never coming back

That part of Mom died it

Turned to ash and blew across the floor or

Maybe it melted and she couldn't
Cup herself through her hands as
Parts of her began seeping
Into the wood and downstairs

A piece of her dripped on my
Shoe as I was tying the laces
I simply wiped it off and
Stood to strap my jacket

See, it was a long time since mother broke
She wasn't used to it
She wasn't as "Resilient" as I was
Didn't use the hospital trips to prepare
Embracing hope instead of
Bracing for despair

I saw the truth, how
Each visit a little less of her
Was in the bed and

More of her in the air

A little less of her was here

And more of her there

These evenings helped me prep the piece

Of her in me for surgery

For the amputation

That would occur any day now

For the guillotine

That would drop without warning

So, when the news came

I was able to neatly sweep

All those shards of glass

Into the garbage pail

I had a basketball game

That part of me was still alive

So I didn't see the point of losing

2 things in one day

And the bus was on its way

13 minutes till arrival

The bus wasn't gonna stop moving

It never stops moving

It never stops moving

It never stops moving

And neither could I

I told my mom I had to go

I already lost 2 minutes

Staring at her blankly

Which left me only 11

To walk to the gate

Well, I really had the full 13

Cus I didn't even go upstairs

I tell people I did so

I can sound more human

And less, like I need counseling

I yelled from the bottom of the stairs,

"I'm leaving"

I could feel her disbelief

Dripping all over me

"Didn't you hear what I said?

Grandma is gone."

I heard

I just didn't want to dwell on it

For I had a father who was still

Alive,

           but dead inside

I mourned his absence

Although he was physically present

For the entirety of my youth

Love me / Dad

Hug me / Dad

Tell me you're proud of me / Dad

Tell me I am enough just as I am / Dad

But the grieving was to no avail

And I learned that no amount of mourning

Could bring a person back

That no matter how many tears you give

It'll be like Magikarp's splash attack

No effect

That once love dies

That's that

I hardly felt anything

As I stared into Grandma's casket

That part of us had already left

From a young age

My father prepared me

To bear a coat of Resilience

For the rest of my life

???

More often

Than I'd like to admit

I find myself

HATING

How bright your smile is how

Effortless your joy seemed

I called *Bullshit!*

Your emotions fake

Unable to fathom

How one could be SO happy

Simply walking to class

I couldn't understand the rays of bliss others seemed to bask in. They HAD to be faking. How could they be happy when there's so much more to be sad about?

It would be another 10 years before I learned that we have the power to control our thoughts.

SELF-FULFILLING PROPHECY

We're taught

That love is weakness

And then wonder

Why we have

So much trouble

Showing

Or receiving it

WERE THERE GOOD TIMES?

There were

I know there were because

Of the memories that other

People share with a smile I

Mirror their facial expressions

Respond generically,

"Yea, that was crazy"

What's crazy is

I'm drawing a blank

When you suppress memories

And erase others the past

Becomes a fish net, only catching

The heavy extremes while those

Blissful moments in between

Slip into the abyss

When you try to erase every mistake

The good times, too,

You're doomed to forget

Memories are fickle things. There were many happy times during these years, and strong friendships forged. However, all I ever focused on were my anxiety and depression, so it's all I remember.

This was made apparent earlier this year, during my high school's 10 year reunion. A classmate offered to do me a SOLID. I was taken aback by the gesture, especially since "I didn't remember us being that close"...I saw the pain in her eyes as the words left my lips. She was confused, voicing otherwise. I was even more confused, but went along with it and made a bullshit excuse as to why I said that.

The next day, her puzzled expression remained in my mind. I tried to plunge into my memories, but could only recall mere moments of our laughs and jokes. I know there was a lot more. I'm pretty sure we got close senior year. But...I really couldn't remember.

Like I said:
If you focus only on the bad, you'll miss out on all the good.

In "Conclusion"

Mountains of appreciation for my cousin, Jon, who pushed me to dive deeper into this period of my life and share without holding back. For helping me make this more than just a book of poems.

Mom and Dad, this collection isn't a shot at you guys. I understand that we all have our flaws, and that we are all suffering in our own ways. It's just that, oftentimes, these struggles manifest negatively towards those we love. Towards the people we share the most with.

For those who can relate to these feelings, if there's only one thing you take from this, let it be the knowledge that:

Y O U   A R E N ' T   A L O N E

Words are the most powerful thing humans have at their disposal. However, they must be SHARED. Otherwise, they are meaningless.

**THANK YOU** for taking this journey with me

For taking the time out of your day to Listen

I'd like to share 3 additional poems about

1) Death

2) Student Loans

and

3) My Hometown

Keep Shining, My Friends
You're Awesome

HALF THE RENT

How much is your life worth?

Half the rent

The room was quiet. Too quiet. Far quieter than I ever thought a room full of these people could ever be

Good

They talk too much, and now isn't the time for that. For the people who always make it about themselves. If Death's chill wasn't hovering in the hallway, their mouths would be flapping incessantly. The room would reek of bullshit as each one unloaded years of guilt. Expired apologies that can't be digested. Half ass stories that can't be dissected; chunks already missing to hide their skeletons.

She lays there looking perfect. A look that betrays her failing organs. I could call her the Bionic Woman, as it's only nuts and bolts keeping her ~~alive~~ here.

Cheating Death
Cheating Life
Why?

Because her SSI pays half the rent. Payment isn't
rendered if you aren't alive. And without life
insurance, it costs more to die. With one foot in the
grave, she sees her sisters who passed before her.
She reaches, but cannot touch, her foot tethered to
the mortal plane by a machine that moves her
lungs for her.

But she can't breathe.

Deceived by these glimpses of Death, because
she's still in the hospital bed. Machines pouring
morphine into her veins. No amount is enough to
dull her spirit's pain. Her sisters hear her screams,
but the land of the living is <u>ignorant</u> of her grief.

Ignorant = Ignoring

Pull the plug, let her die. How much are these
painful days really worth?

Half the rent

Don't give her those crocodile tears. It's not sorrow, but selfish. If you really loved her, you'd let her go. I'm not sure if it's fear, or finances, that justifies this decision to keep her plugged into the Matrix. Face it! You and I both know it's her time. But you're too worried about what comes next. Like:

"How will I pay the rent?"

TRAPPED

When I was a boy my favorite cousin

(favorite just means he was the only cousin I saw
often cus momma was so afraid of the past she
escaped catching a whiff of her scent and burning
her freedom papers that she unconsciously
equated her family with the ghetto)

So, my cousin

Got so hiiiigh he never came back down

Or, as momma likes to put it,

"He got so loooooww he never came back up"

Like the top of the water froze while he was skinny
dipping but he didn't realize he was trapped. He
somehow grew gills and forgot he ever lived on
land, so he never had a reason to come up for air

Momma says that's what happens when good
people stay where they don't belong (the hood) for
too long. It transforms them into something they
aren't   is that why you

left and didn't come back is that why you   broke your back to send me to privileged schools no matter the cost   but momma sometimes I think I would have been safer in the hood cus despite the dangers there these places you sent me were ruthless. There they equate my culture with news headlines and *bang bang shoot em up* music   I can't tell you how many people were shocked by my lack of known facts about rap music and told me I wasn't really black but...melanin ain't an act STUPID. The sum of MY culture isn't YOUR entertainment and when I tried to wake them they kept pressing snooze, ignoring my painful truths and labeling them as radical, ungrateful views cus

"It's 2008, black people have it good now"

"It's 2016, they got mad opportunities"

Staying in the hood too long might have changed me like cousin Jeff but spending 8 years here made me think my voice didn't matter cus no one wants to discuss how race is a factor or that violence isn't what my brothers are after   it's really *Love*

A hunger for validation that drives us to these sticky situations   momma what I'm trying say is being here changed me, too. I wish for once you'd stop worshipping these schools as if they were the hand and I was the tool lucky enough to be pulled from the shelf cus out there,

Niggas fly so high they never wanna come back down

Not to say niggas belong on the ground but from time to time you gotta touch down. We ain't like these rich folk in these schools daddy can just drop a donation to get them out of their sticky situations so justice is money ?   And if I react to the hate they spew *I'm* the aggressor when I'm just trying to teach 'em how to treat people better cus we're all children of the same Father…but they'll make you feel like yo momma was the mistress aka the maid raped in the kitchen and then paid in tuition to sweep it under the rug

To the snow bunnies, I'm that stray dog they love feeding pussy to, but will never bring home because they don't want mud or the smell of a life they ain't used to on their marble floors

Taking $160k in loans for my bachelors only to search for job prospects rarer than magic rarer than the steak on the plate of the old white man raking in the cake he makes off the American dream he sold to high schools.

Shiiiiit he got that Scrooge McDuck money while I'm pinching pennies cus my checks were garnished—Sallie says that's what happens when too many payments are late

Momma,   you said education was an investment but to me this a poor business plan like trying to give fish legs knowing they can't breathe on land or building a baseball field in Alaska. I understand you wanted to give me an opportunity you never had, but all I learned were the rules to a game I'll never be allowed to play, at least not on equal footing. Shouldn't we work on changing this system?

Cus I'm *still* waiting for the future I paid for

Or are you trapped momma

Like cousin Jeff

And just don't know it...

Abandoned

Ode to Staten Island

We stand in the ruins of truth, cus lies were the only things that carried us this far. And once we ran out of those, everything else fell apart. It's hard trusting humans with my heart.

I just want people to like me

If they did, it'd be a lot easier to like myself. Don't mean to seem sneaky, but I'm not a fan of full disclosure, too used to people walking away when the weight of those words saturate the air with my troubles.

I know a lot about being abandoned, it's ingrained in my city. The "forgotten borough" rarely mentioned by his 4 siblings, as if Staten Island were birthed by a different mother. The unacknowledged kin who's a reminder of all the things they aren't. Or, maybe, all the things they used to be.

And what about graduation? When I returned
home old homies looked at me different, with a
mix of

1) wishing they got "chose"

2) envy that these streets ain't turn my heart cold

3) and disgust

Cus to them I sold my soul   sometimes I think I
did and it wasn't nearly enough so Sallie Mae took
an interest in covering my gamble so that she could
collect interest and rip my credit score to shambles
a degree,   is bait on the lure of equal
opportunity, cus they know niggas looooove
chasing that paper

What's the craziest thing you ever did to get paid?

Rob a bank?

Shiiiit that ain't crazy you had a guarantee the
money was in the vault and that you'd more than
quadruple back what you spent on the operation

Me?

Is that what you see when you look at me?
Mistakes?

A cluster of "things gone wrong" or "too far gone"?

We're tired of feeling like a pit stop. A space to
entertain for a brief reprieve, then quickly
forgotten as you ride off towards where you really
wanna be.

Just once I'd like to be the destination. Not a
combination of wrong turns + reluctance to ask for
directions. WHAT CAN I DO TO CHANGE THAT?

My superpower became deleting memories, as
they only brought grief.

However, history must be observed, not ignored.
Without these lessons, I fell prey to repeating the
same mistakes, making change impossible.

The desperation to erase ALL pain, to seem
"normal", prevented meaningful connections from
taking root. My actions were haunted by the
people who left, overshadowing those who stayed.
Instead of keeping it real, life became trying to live

up to the ideals I thought OTHERS would find appealing.

"Friends", are worse than prison when you're dishonest about your interests, and play ride-a-long with theirs. Hiding who you are is never worth it. *Shine*! And fuck what anyone has to say. By trying to make people like me, I missed out on the ones who would have loved me.

Yea, I've been abandoned, but I'm no longer defined by those who left, nor should I forget them. Enjoy every experience to the fullest, no matter how long or how little it lasts. You can't create a brighter future, until you embrace the pain in your past.

MATTHEW FIGUEROA provides supportive/therapeutic services to individuals with developmental and/or mental diagnoses. He has been featured at various NYC events for his poetry & music. Matthew's debut collection of poems is fueled by the anxiety and depression he struggled with in high school. He currently holds a B.A. in Psychology from Wesleyan University, and a MS in Special Education from Touro College.

Instagram: @The_Invincible_Figgz

Matfigueroa12@gmail.com

Made in the USA
Middletown, DE
26 January 2019